Giant Pandas

by Michelle Levine

Lerner Publications Company • Minneapolis

Lerner Publications Company
A division of Lerner Publishing Group
241 First Avenue North
Minneapolis, MN 55401

Website address: www.lernerbooks.com

Words in *italic* type are explained in a glossary on page 30.

Library of Congress Cataloging-in-Publication Data

Levine, Michelle.
    Giant pandas / by Michelle Levine.
      p.   cm. — (Pull ahead books)
    Includes index.
    ISBN-13: 978-0-8225-3482-2 (lib. bdg. : alk. paper)
    ISBN-10: 0-8225-3482-7 (lib. bdg. : alk. paper)
    1. Giant panda—Juvenile literature. I. Title. II. Series.
  QL737.C214L48 2006
  599.789—dc22   2005010673

Manufactured in the United States of America
1 2 3 4 5 6 — JR — 11 10 09 08 07 06

This bear is black and white and furry all over.

What kind of bear is it?

This bear is a giant panda.

Giant pandas live
in the mountains of China.

These mountains are cold.

A panda's fur keeps it warm
and dry in the mountains.

Which parts of the panda
have black fur?

A panda has black fur
around its eyes and on its ears.

Its legs and shoulders are black too.

Giant pandas spend a lot of time *browsing* in the forest.

Browsing means feeding on plants.

A browsing panda
feeds on *bamboo*.

A panda uses its front paws to grab
and hold the bamboo.

CRUNCH!

The panda uses its strong jaws
and teeth to chew the bamboo.

Pandas need to eat a lot
of bamboo to stay healthy.

They also need fresh water.

Pandas drink from mountain creeks and streams.

Pandas take short naps
between eating and drinking.

Sometimes they sleep against trees.

Young pandas climb trees
to stay away from danger.

How else are trees important
to pandas?

A panda can sniff a tree to find out
if another panda is nearby.

Pandas rub trees
to leave their scent.

The scent tells
other pandas,
"I was here!"

Mother pandas sometimes make their *dens* inside large trees.

A den is a safe place.

Baby pandas are born in dens.
A baby panda is called a *cub*.

A newborn cub is pink and tiny.
It is as small as a stick of butter!

Soon it grows warm fur.

The cub *nurses* to grow
big and strong.

It drinks
milk from its
mother.

A growing cub does not leave
its den for four or five months.

The mother stays with her cub
in the den.

She leaves only for short trips
to browse.

This cub has left its den. But the cub stays close to its mother.

The mother and cub make sounds to keep in touch.

Pandas honk, growl, and squeak.

This cub is about one year old.
It can eat bamboo.

It can climb trees.

Soon it will be a grown-up
giant panda!

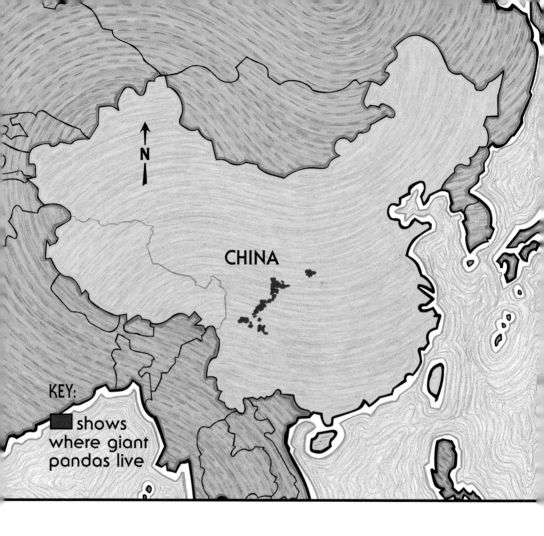

This is a map of China.
Where do giant pandas live?

Parts of a Giant Panda's Body

head

fur

ear

tail

eye

nose

mouth

front
leg

claw

paw

back
leg

Glossary

bamboo: a kind of grass that has hard stems, green leaves, and juicy shoots

browsing: feeding on plants

cub: a baby giant panda

dens: safe places where mother pandas live with their cubs

nurses: drinks mother's milk

Further Reading and Websites

Donaldson, Madeline. *Asia*. Minneapolis: Lerner
Publications Company, 2005. Learn about Asia, the
huge continent where giant pandas live.

Bears at Enchanted Learning
http://www.enchantedlearning.com/themes/bear.shtml
This site has information about giant pandas and other
kinds of bears, as well as crafts, quizzes, and printouts to
color.

Giant Pandas—National Zoo
http://nationalzoo.si.edu/Animals/GiantPandas/
Find out all about the giant pandas at the National Zoo
in Washington, D.C., then watch them on the
PandaCam!

Index

Photo Acknowledgments

The photographs in this book are reproduced with permission from:
© CORBIS SYGMA, front cover; © Keren Su/CORBIS, p. 3; © Keren
Su/China Span, pp. 4, 5, 6, 7, 8, 9, 10, 11, 12, 13, 14, 15, 16, 17, 18,
19, 20, 21, 22, 23, 24, 25, 26, 27, 30.